GW00501315

Jacqueline Wilson

ILLUSTRATED BY NICK SHARRATT

Diary
2016

DOUBLEDAY

THIS DIARY BELONGS TO:

Here's a
photo of me!

Name: _Caoimhe_

Address: ~~20 Park Road~~
~~Muskry Estat~~
87 Green Filds Baillingolig
Fermoulk Co, Cork

Phone number: ~~086 8763539~~
02

Email: _____

Birthday: _1 June_

WHAT'S YOUR FAVOURITE ANIMAL?

There are so many to choose from!
You might pick a sleek, beautiful
horse or a fierce, growling wolf. You
could go for a great, big elephant with
giant, flapping ears, or a cheeky, playful monkey –
like Mavis, who Hetty Feather meets at Tanglefield's
Travelling Circus! You could choose a beautiful
butterfly, like Tina in *The Butterfly Club*. Or what
about a soft, fluffy cat? There are
lots of cats in Jacqueline Wilson's
books, like *Queenie* and
The Cat Mummy – which
might give you a clue
about Jacqueline's own
favourite animal!

Write all about your favourite animal on the
following pages. You could even draw a picture,
stick in a picture you've cut out of a magazine,
or paste in a photograph you took yourself!

Horse

dog

AMAZING ANIMALS

Animals fall into one of five categories: mammals, reptiles, amphibians, fish and birds. (Insects are classed in a different way.) You can work out what category any animal falls into by answering a few simple questions. If an animal is warm-blooded and has fur or hair, it's a mammal. If it's warm-blooded with feathers and wings, and lays eggs, it is a bird. Cold-blooded creatures with dry skin and scales are reptiles, while cold-blooded animals with moist skin and webbed feet are amphibians. Finally, cold-blooded animals with scales and fins which live and breathe underwater (using gills, not lungs) are fish!

DID YOU KNOW . . .

Tortoises can live up to 150 years old!
The oldest tortoise ever, Tui Malila, lived to
be an amazing 188 years old.

Sharks are at the top of the food chain in the
ocean, and they've been around for a very
long time. Sharks were swimming around even
before dinosaurs roamed the earth.
That's old!

There are two kinds of elephant: Indian, and African.
They look very similar, but there are ways of telling
the difference between them: African elephants have
larger ears and a rounder head with a domed top,
while Indian elephants have a slight dip in the middle
of their heads. Plus, only male Asian elephants
grow tusks, whereas both male and female
African elephants do.

The largest member of the cat family is the tiger. Unlike lots of other cats, wild tigers are good swimmers, and will happily cool off in lakes or streams during hot weather.

Above any other type of food, pandas love to eat bamboo, but it's very low in nutrition, so they have to eat lots of it – meaning a panda can spend up to 16 hours a day eating just to get enough energy!

The tiny hummingbirds are the only birds able to fly backwards.

There are around 3000 types of snake in the world. The tiniest is the thread snake, which grows to about 10 centimetres in length, and looks a lot like a harmless earthworm that you might find in your garden!

The first animal to travel into space was a dog. Laika was a Russian stray, who was trained for her space mission along with two other dogs, Albina and Mushka. She was very brave and intelligent.

PUZZLES!

There are lots of different names for groups of animals. You've probably heard of 'a herd of elephants' before, and 'a litter of kittens'.

Can you match up some of these unusual grouping names with the right animals?

1. A pride of   **a.** Hyenas

2. A school of   **b.** Camels

3. A tower of   **c.** Fish

4. An unkindness of   **d.** Rhinos

5. A swarm of   **e.** Ravens

6. A crash of   **f.** Bees

7. A caravan of   **g.** Lions

8. A cackle of   **h.** Giraffes

There are twelve animals hidden in this jumble
of letters. You'll find them listed across, backwards,
up, down and diagonally. As a clue, here are
the letters they each begin with!

- ★ F
- ★ O
- ★ B
- ★ S
- ★ H
- ★ P
- ★ P
- ★ G
- ★ W
- ★ R
- ★ S
- ★ F

V	H	F	J	K	A	J	G	W	X	O	I	L	P	N	U
B	S	D	H	U	F	R	E	Q	Z	K	F	B	N	U	J
A	R	H	I	N	O	C	E	R	O	S	E	V	L	I	K
F	L	T	B	U	R	M	A	Y	Q	W	B	U	O	K	T
R	E	K	A	N	S	I	D	N	M	H	L	S	E	N	E
H	R	R	A	W	E	L	N	S	O	A	N	I	I	G	A
U	R	D	O	O	G	E	A	H	T	L	I	U	O	O	S
D	I	P	L	A	T	Y	P	U	S	E	L	H	O	K	G
G	J	S	O	F	L	E	N	R	M	I	L	R	T	L	B
U	Q	A	R	A	K	B	U	K	T	S	S	S	R	O	R
R	S	G	L	N	C	U	T	N	O	R	Y	D	I	M	Q
F	O	A	B	O	O	N	R	O	F	U	H	K	L	P	U
E	S	H	J	E	R	T	U	I	F	S	G	H	F	O	W
N	D	P	O	I	E	R	Q	A	T	J	D	J	F	M	O

You'll find the answers at the back of this diary!

TIMETABLE

Fill in your lessons here – and don't forget
your after-school clubs and practices.

TIME	MONDAY	TUESDAY
8.30		
9.00		
9.30		
10.00		
10.30		
11.00		
11.30		
12.00		
12.30		
1.00		
1.30		
2.00		
2.30		
3.00		
3.30		
4.00		
4.30		
5.00		
5.30		

TIMETABLE

Fill in your lessons here – and don't forget
your after-school clubs and practices.

WEDNESDAY	THURSDAY	FRIDAY
Drama		

JANUARY

I knelt down and cautiously lifted the box lid a few inches. I peered into the darkness inside. There was a lot of soft straw. Huddled right in the middle, ears twitching anxiously, was a little grey rabbit.

COOKIE

Monday 28 December

Tuesday 29 December

Wednesday 30 December

New years eve.
up to Galway (Yippy)

Thursday 31 December

New year

Friday 1 January

Saturday 2 January

Sunday 3 January

Nana + Poppys
in Limrik
cant wait
and goaing
home

Monday 4 January

Tuesday 5 January

Party in Bowns zoo

ahling Darby Party

Wednesday 6 January

Back to schol. I hate schol.

Thursday 7 January

Friday 8 January

Saturday 9 January

Sunday 10 January

Notes

Monday 11 January

Tuesday 12 January

Wednesday 13 January

Thursday 14 January

Friday 15 January

Saturday 16 January

Broghnas birthday

Sunday 17 January

Broghnas Party

Notes
I dident get an
invit to Broghnas
Party

Monday 18 January

Tuesday 19 January

Wednesday 20 January

Thursday 21 January

Friday 22 January

Saturday 23 January

Éabhas Birthday
Party

Sunday 24 January

Notes

Monday 25 January

Tuesday 26 January

Wednesday 27 January

Thursday 28 January

Srenas party
Baltte

Friday 29 January

Saturday 30 January

Sunday 31 January

Notes

FEBRUARY

I settled to drawing my Adonis blue butterfly, and then I selected the bright
blue pencil from my tin. I coloured it in ever so carefully, making
the blue darker near the wing tips, and leaving a white
fringe all round the edges of the wings. Even the
Adonis blue's body was blue and very furry.

THE BUTTERFLY CLUB

Monday 1 February

Tuesday 2 February

Wednesday 3 February

Thursday 4 February

Friday 5 February

Kery and
Thaghs
Birthday

Saturday 6 February

Sunday 7 February

Monday 8 February

Tuesday 9 February

Pankae Tuesday

Wednesday 10 February

ash   W.   Kerys party

fun Bus

Thursday 11 February

Friday 12 February

Saturday 13 February

Sunday 14 February

Notes

Monday 15 February

Tuesday 16 February

Wednesday 17 February

Thursday 18 February

Friday 19 February

Sporty Scary Baby Posh

Saturday 20 February

Sunday 21 February

Dustbin Licky

Notes

Monday 22 February

Tuesday 23 February

Wednesday 24 February

Thursday 25 February

Friday 26 February

Saturday 27 February

Sunday 28 February

Notes

MARCH

I sat up straight as six sleek horses cantered into the ring. I was used to Dobbin and Rowley, the great shire horses in Father's care at the farm. These dancing, prancing horses seemed an elvish breed, so small and dainty. Two were spotted, two piebald and two grey, all with their manes and tails flowing, long and silky.

HETTY FEATHER

Monday 29 February

Tuesday 1 March

Wednesday 2 March

Thursday 3 March

Friday 4 March

Saturday 5 March

Sunday 6 March

Monday 7 March

Tuesday 8 March

Wednesday 9 March

Thursday 10 March

Friday 11 March

Saturday 12 March

Sunday 13 March

Notes

Monday 14 March

Tuesday 15 March

Wednesday 16 March

Thursday 17 March

Friday 18 March

Saturday 19 March

Sunday 20 March

Notes

Monday 21 March

Tuesday 22 March

Wednesday 23 March

Thursday 24 March

Friday 25 March

Saturday 26 March

Sunday 27 March

Notes

APRIL

Miss Anderson starts talking about food chains. 'From the tiniest shrimp to the biggest whale, all living things play roles in the food chain,' she says. I draw a tiny shrimp on the back of my roughbook. It's hunched up and wrinkled, a bit like Samson. Then I draw an enormous mouth and huge teeth. It's open wide, ready to gobble up the shrimp.

THE LONGEST WHALE SONG

Monday 28 March

Tuesday 29 March

Wednesday 30 March

Thursday 31 March

Friday 1 April

Saturday 2 April

Sunday 3 April

Monday 4 April

Tuesday 5 April

Wednesday 6 April

Thursday 7 April

Friday 8 April

Saturday 9 April

Sunday 10 April

Notes

Monday 11 April

Tuesday 12 April

Wednesday 13 April

Thursday 14 April

Friday 15 April

Saturday 16 April

Sunday 17 April

Notes

Monday 18 April

Tuesday 19 April

Wednesday 20 April

Thursday 21 April

Friday 22 April

Saturday 23 April

Sunday 24 April

Notes

Monday 25 April

Tuesday 26 April

Wednesday 27 April

Thursday 28 April

Friday 29 April

Saturday 30 April

Sunday 1 May
Moms Birthday

Notes

MAY

I saw a gigantic grey head poking up above the hedge – a *huge* head with wrinkled skin and a tiny eye and the longest nose in all the world. I knew what it was! 'Oh my stars! E is for *Elephant!*' I gasped.

HETTY FEATHER

Monday 2 May

Tuesday 3 May

Wednesday 4 May

Thursday 5 May

Friday 6 May

Saturday 7 May

Sunday 8 May

Monday 9 May

Tuesday 10 May

Wednesday 11 May

Thursday 12 May

Friday 13 May

Saturday 14 May

Sunday 15 May

Notes

Monday 16 May

Tuesday 17 May

Wednesday 18 May

B
b

Thursday 19 May

Orlas   Birthday
(my sister)

Friday 20 May

Saturday 21 May

Sunday 22 May

Notes

Monday 23 May

Tuesday 24 May

Wednesday 25 May

Thursday 26 May

Friday 27 May

Saturday 28 May

Sunday 29 May

Notes

JUNE

I'd have given anything for a proper pet, though not necessarily something fluffy. A real porcupine would be ultra-cool. Or a turtle who could live in the bath. Or a hyena that laughed at my jokes.

THE WORST THING ABOUT MY SISTER

_____

Monday 30 May

_____

Tuesday 31 May

_____

Wednesday 1 June

Caoimhe s (me) Birthday

Thursday 2 June

Friday 3 June

Saturday 4 June

Sunday 5 June

Monday 6 June

Tuesday 7 June

Wednesday 8 June

Thursday 9 June

Friday 10 June

Saturday 11 June

Sunday 12 June

Notes

Monday 13 June

Tuesday 14 June

Wednesday 15 June

Thursday 16 June

Friday 17 June

Saturday 18 June

Sunday 19 June

Notes

Monday 20 June

_____

Tuesday 21 June

_____

Wednesday 22 June

_____

Thursday 23 June

Friday 24 June

Saturday 25 June

Sunday 26 June

Notes

Monday 27 June

Tuesday 28 June

Wednesday 29 June

Thursday 30 June

JULY

I found the photo of Jenna Williams with her kitten. I copied Lulu very carefully, and then coloured my picture with my best felt tips. I spent ages with the grey pen, inking in hundreds of little dashes to make the kitten look extra furry.

PAWS AND WHISKERS

Friday 1 July

Saturday 2 July

Sunday 3 July

Monday 4 July

Tuesday 5 July

Wednesday 6 July

Thursday 7 July

Friday 8 July

Saturday 9 July

Sunday 10 July

Notes

Monday 11 July

Tuesday 12 July

Wednesday 13 July

Thursday 14 July

Friday 15 July

Saturday 16 July

Sunday 17 July

Notes

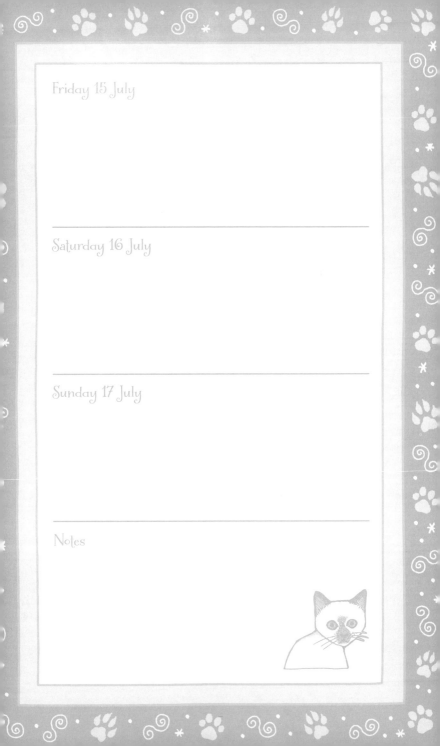

Monday 18 July

Tuesday 19 July

Padrigs Birtholay

Wednesday 20 July

Thursday 21 July

Friday 22 July

Saturday 23 July

Sunday 24 July

Notes

Monday 25 July

Tuesday 26 July

Wednesday 27 July

Thursday 28 July

Friday 29 July

Saturday 30 July

Sunday 31 July

Notes

AUGUST

I clapped so hard my hands stung. I watched
the monkeys and the lions, and the performing
seals and the astonishingly huge elephant,
marvelling at them all.

DIAMOND

Monday 1 August

Tuesday 2 August

Wednesday 3 August

Thursday 4 August

Friday 5 August

Saturday 6 August

Sunday 7 August

Monday 8 August

Tuesday 9 August

Wednesday 10 August

Thursday 11 August

Friday 12 August

Saturday 13 August

Sunday 14 August

Notes

Monday 15 August

Tuesday 16 August

Wednesday 17 August

Thursday 18 August

Friday 19 August

Saturday 20 August

Sunday 21 August

Notes

Monday 22 August

Tuesday 23 August

Wednesday 24 August

Thursday 25 August

Friday 26 August

Saturday 27 August

Sunday 28 August

Notes

Monday 29 August

Tuesday 30 August

Wednesday 31 August

Back to school yaa (not)

Thursday 1 September

SEPTEMBER

I took my sketchbook out of my satchel and looked at all my
beautiful butterflies. I read about the flowers they liked
to feed on. I ached to make a butterfly garden
so that I could watch them fluttering about my
very own flowers. I wanted to make it myself.

THE BUTTERFLY CLUB

Friday 2 September

Saturday 3 September

Sunday 4 September

Monday 5 September

Tuesday 6 September

Wednesday 7 September

Thursday 8 September

Friday 9 September

Saturday 10 September

Sunday 11 September

Notes

Monday 12 September

Tuesday 13 September

Wednesday 14 September

Thursday 15 September

Friday 16 September

Saturday 17 September

Sunday 18 September

Notes

Monday 19 September

Tuesday 20 September

Today was Eimers birthday.
She brout in jelleys

Wednesday 21 September

Nana and poppy coma
down

Thursday 22 September

Friday 23 September

We are moving house

Saturday 24 September

Nana and Poppy go home

Sunday 25 September

Eoniars Party can't waite in aseme wall at 12 am - 2 pm

Notes

I can't wate because I am going with Eaniar.

Yaadera meeting Eniar

Monday 26 September

Today Patrick brot buns in. They wher yum!

Tuesday 27 September

Aishling is comeing over. Yaaaaa

Wednesday 28 September

We did art today!

Thursday 29 September

I fourd my Coimunin presents.

OCTOBER

'You just like cute and cuddly animals, I want a
really exciting pet,' I said. My head felt like
a Noah's Ark as animals of all shapes
and sizes trumpeted and roared
and whinnied in my mind.

BIG DAY OUT

Friday 30 September

Lucky day
I won the rafle. We won best
table. me and Edha won the
thin whistle. Lucky charm

Saturday 1 October

Poppy and Garver
comeing down. Yha
They shoud be down
at 11:00.

Sunday 2 October

Monday 3 October

Tuesday 4 October

Wednesday 5 October

got a lot of *homew*
ork. 😊

Thursday 6 October

I think I did well
in my test

Friday 7 October

Saturday 8 October

Squirrel
Monkey

Sunday 9 October

I wonder what my
ousults are.

Notes

Cinistifer
has a bit of a
crush on me !!

Monday 10 October

Kate wasn't in
school. 😶

Tuesday 11 October

Wednesday 12 October

Thursday 13 October

Dabs Birthday

Friday 14 October

Saturday 15 October

Sunday 16 October

Notes

Monday 17 October

Tuesday 18 October

Wednesday 19 October

Thursday 20 October

Friday 21 October

today was so
good

Saturday 22 October

Sunday 23 October

Notes

Monday 24 October

Tuesday 25 October

Wednesday 26 October

Thursday 27 October

Friday 28 October

Saturday 29 October

Sunday 30 October

Notes

NOVEMBER

I started to help cage the troupe of performing
monkeys, and loved packing up all their props
and tiny costumes. I adored the monkeys –
especially little Mavis, the baby.

DIAMOND

Monday 31 October

Tuesday 1 November

Wednesday 2 November

Thursday 3 November

Friday 4 November

Saturday 5 November

Sunday 6 November

Monday 7 November

Tuesday 8 November

Wednesday 9 November

Thursday 10 November

Friday 11 November

Saturday 12 November

Sunday 13 November

Notes

Monday 14 November

Tuesday 15 November

Wednesday 16 November

Thursday 17 November

Friday 18 November

Saturday 19 November

Sunday 20 November

Notes

Monday 21 November

Tuesday 22 November

Wednesday 23 November

Thursday 24 November

Friday 25 November

Saturday 26 November

Sunday 27 November

Notes

Monday 28 November

Tuesday 29 November

Wednesday 30 November

Thursday 1 December

DECEMBER

I put my hand out, trembling, and felt the softest fur, like thistledown.
I stroked tentatively, and the cat started purring, rubbing her head
under my hand, clearly telling me to keep on stroking. I held her
with one hand and stroked with the other, from her head all the
way down her body to the tip of her long tail.

QUEENIE

Friday 2 December

Saturday 3 December

Sunday 4 December

Monday 5 December

Tuesday 6 December

Wednesday 7 December

Thursday 8 December

Friday 9 December

Saturday 10 December

Sunday 11 December

Notes

Monday 12 December

Tuesday 13 December

Wednesday 14 December

Thursday 15 December

Friday 16 December

Tomáses Birthday

Saturday 17 December

Sunday 18 December

Notes

Monday 19 December

Tuesday 20 December

Wednesday 21 December

Thursday 22 December

Friday 23 December

Saturday 24 December

Sunday 25 December

Notes

Monday 26 December

Tuesday 27 December

Wednesday 28 December

Thursday 29 December

Friday 30 December

Saturday 31 December

Sunday 1 January

Notes

PHOTO ALBUM!

Why not stick your favourite photos or draw
your favourite moments from 2016 here!

PUZZLE ANSWERS!

8a. A cackle of hyenas

7b. A caravan of camels

6d. A crash of rhinos

5f. A swarm of bees

4e. An unkindness of ravens

3h. A tower of giraffes

2c. A school of fish

1g. A pride of lions

Have you seen this other gorgeous stationery?

THE JACQUELINE WILSON DIARY 2016
A DOUBLEDAY BOOK 978 0 857 53199 5

Published in Great Britain by Doubleday,
an imprint of Random House Children's Books
A Penguin Random House Company

Penguin
Random House
UK

This edition published 2015

1 3 5 7 9 10 8 6 4 2

Copyright © Jacqueline Wilson, 2007, 2015
Illustrations copyright © Nick Sharratt, 2007, 2015

Penguin Random House is committed to a sustainable future for our
business, our readers and our planet. This book is made from
Forest Stewardship Council ® certified paper.

MIX
Paper from
responsible sources
FSC® C018179

Set in Liam

RANDOM HOUSE CHILDREN'S PUBLISHERS UK
61-63 Uxbridge Road, London W5 5SA

www.randomhousechildrens.co.uk
www.totallyrandombooks.co.uk
www.randomhouse.co.uk

Addresses for companies within The Random House Group Limited
can be found at: www.randomhouse.co.uk/offices.htm

THE RANDOM HOUSE GROUP Limited Reg. No. 954009

A CIP catalogue record for this book is available from the British Library.

Printed and bound in China